With love
from
Rarlene
to
Maia Jane

LITTLE ☆ STARS™

TAURUS

A parent's guide to the little star of the family

JOHN ASTROP

with illustrations by the author

E L E M E N T

Shaftesbury, Dorset ● Rockport, Massachusetts
Brisbane, Queensland

Published in Great Britain in 1994 by
Element Books Ltd.
Longmead, Shaftesbury, Dorset

Published in the USA in 1994 by
Element, Inc.
42 Broadway, Rockport, MA 01966

Published in Australia in 1994 by
Element Books Ltd.
for Jacaranda Wiley Ltd.
33 Park Road, Milton, Brisbane, 4064

Printed and bound in Great Britain by
BPC Paulton Books Ltd.

British Library Cataloguing in Publication
data available

Library of Congress Cataloguing in publication
data available

ISBN 1-85230-538-X

CONTENTS

THE TWELVE SIGNS

Everyone knows a little about the twelve sun signs. It's the easiest way to approach real astrology without going to the trouble of casting up a chart for the exact time of birth. You won't learn everything about a person with the sun sign but you'll know a lot more than if you just use observation and guesswork. The sun is in roughly the same sign and degree of the zodiac at the same time every year. It's a nice astronomical event that doesn't need calculating. So if you're born between

May 22 and June 21 you'll be pretty sure you're a Gemini; between June 22 and July 23 then you're a Cancer and so on. Many people say how can you divide the human race into twelve sections and are there only twelve different types. Well for a start most people make assessments and judgements on their fellow humans with far smaller groups than that. Rich and poor, educated and non-educated, town girl, country boy, etc. Even with these very simple pigeon holes we can combine to make 'Rich educated town boy' and 'poor non-educated country girl'. We try to get as much information as we can about the others that we make relationships with through life. Astrology as a way of describing and understanding others is unsurpassed. Take the traditional meaning of the twelve signs:

Aries - is self-assertive, brave, energetic and pioneering.

Taurus - is careful, possessive, values material things, is able to build and make things grow.

Gemini - is bright-minded, curious, communicative and versatile.

Cancer - is sensitive, family orientated, protective and caring.

Leo - is creative, dramatic, a leader, showy and generous.

Virgo - is organised, critical, perfectionist and practical.

Libra - is balanced, diplomatic, harmonious, sociable, and likes beautiful things.

Scorpio - is strong-willed, magnetic, powerful, extreme, determined and recuperative.

Sagittarius - is adventurous, philosophical, far-thinking, blunt, truth-seeking.

Capricorn - is cautious, responsible, patient, persistent and ambitious.

Aquarius - is rebellious, unorthodox, humanitarian, idealistic, a fighter of good causes.

Pisces - is sensitive, imaginative, caring, visionary and sacrificing.

If you can find anyone in your circle of friends and acquaintances who isn't described pretty neatly by one of the above it would be surprising. Put the twelve signs into different lives and occupations and you see how it works. A Taurean priest would be more likely to devote his life to looking after the physical and material needs of his church members, feeding the poor, setting up charities. A Virgoan bank robber would plan meticulously and never commit spontaneous crimes. A Leo teacher would make learning an entertainment and a pleasure for her pupils.

So with parents and children. A Capricorn child handles the business of growing up and learning in a very different way to a Libran child. A Scorpio parent manages the family quite differently to an Aquarian. The old boast, 'I'm very fair, I treat all my children the same', may not be the best way to help your little ones at all. Our individual drive is the key to making a success of life. The time when we need the most acceptance of the way we are is in childhood. As a parent it's good to know the ways in which our little ones are like us but we must never forget the ways in which they are different.

LITTLE TAURUS

You're going to thank your lucky stars now you've got one of these little fellahs in the family. Calm as can be and don't they just love all the cuddling and loving that you can't resist giving 'em. They like their food, they like their sleep, in fact they are just the most ideal new member to add to the family. That is until.... Yes, you've probably discovered already that little Bulls love doing what they want to do but that's all! Once a Taurean, no matter how tiny, feels she is being forced into something new, something different or just something she doesn't like, then the first great impasse comes into your life. No matter how you fancy your chances at cajoling and gentle persuasion, you're going to fail miserably! Taureans like what they know they like. They try out things for themselves slowly and once they have made a decision, come what may, they stick to it. Moving on to the next experiment may seem to you to take an eternity. In fact they are not great movers at all. While their friends are galloping hither and thither bruising knees, grazing elbows and generally creating havoc, you'll find little Taurus calmly sitting down exploring the texture of an old well-squeezed bread roll he's been carrying round since lunch. When it gets soft enough, he'll probably  mould and fashion it into a passable if slightly surrealist portrait sculpture of his teddy bear. Good with their hands little Bulls, in fact the great Salvador Dali was a notable one. This ability to explore and understand the essence of material things is the main reason that Taureans seem so painfully slow to learn anything and even slower to move on to the next project. Taurus is an Earth sign and it is the nature of earth to nourish small seeds into tender shoots and maintain their strength to grow into healthy plants and glorious blossom. You can't rush the process if you want to guarantee a good crop and so with your little Taurus. Actions mean more to them than words and love is, more often than not, shown by a material or physical demonstration of affection. They are much more likely to grow up to be the one that sends a dozen red roses to a lover rather than whisper sweet nothings in a shell-like ear. When Junior helps with the dishwashing or brings you her first 'made all by myself' tepid cup of coffee this will be genuine love. Although easily falling into the habit of lolling around indoors, little Taurus responds to his own element earth with beneficial effects. Plenty of trips to the great outdoors where the grass is green and the foliage luxuriant and your sluggish little plodder will skip lightly and happily, appreciating the earthiness and the beauty of the countryside. A big town park will do the job just as well! The old Walt Disney cartoon of the little Bull that didn't want to fight but loved flowers wasn't far off the easygoing Taurean character.

THE BABY

The chances are that this calm little babe will have made for a fairly easy pregnancy, as few Taurean babes waste a lot of time and energy kicking when they can just lie there comfortably. On arrival in this strange world the first reaction may turn out to be an anticlimax of long hours of sleep and little of the arm flailing and experimental claw-ing of more hyperactive babies. After the first week or so you won't mind not being awakened at all hours and you'll love the fact that this little one seems to settle quickly to routine times for everything. How easy things are and what an ideal baby all your friends will say. True, this cute small package will delight you with her calm satisfaction and happy gurgles until the moment that you begin to worry, 'Shouldn't she be trying to grab things?' 'Don't you think she should have tried crawling by now?' Forget right away the business of comparing your infant's speed of growth and achievements with mums of more precocious brats, your little wonder has started the way she means to go on. In her own time!

THE FIRST THREE YEARS

The Taurus baby will certainly be a late crawler and even if you have produced the one in three that does manage to move a little earlier you won't have too many worries about little Taurus getting into mischief. Sitting on the carpet just where you put him half an hour ago, your little Bull is quite happy to stay there all day sorting over his pile of familiar toys between his pudgy legs, provided, of course, the regular doses of lovely grub and warm drinks come at the expected times. You'll notice this babe takes a real pleasure in food but once her tastes have been made clear, she won't respond very well to your desire to provide a broad and varied diet. Trying out new foods is a slow process and even if you manage to get it into the unsuspecting mouth you'll end up with a finely food-sprayed sweater in seconds. Little Bulls can sometimes become infuriatingly unadventurous where their diet is concerned and you may have to face the problem of providing the same two jars of baby food wherever you go whatever the circumstance.

Taureans like regularity and with any luck and a bit of good timing on your part you both should be able to deal easily with the potty training period. As Junior develops more self-confidence and mobility the need for self-expression and development  of true Taurean artistic talents may put you in for some surprise artworks. An interesting abstract treatment on the leg of the kitchen table with Mom's lipstick; the lounge wall improved with a sketchy raspberry jelly landscape. Take the hint, put down the newspaper, add plenty of finger paints, modelling clay and overalls (this little one simply loves getting messy!) and let art rule!

THE KINDERGARTEN

Gently shoving this one into the big world outside home is not always easy and it may have been good foresight to have invited little friends round regularly in the six months or so prior to start of play school. Little Taureans are not only possessive with their toys but also with their small friends. This can cause constant little dramas when the hustle and bustle of this all-child environment becomes a reality. If the adored teddy he brought gets 'borrowed' by little Tom or his 'very best ever friend' goes off and plays with nasty ol' David then the next

visit will take a lifetime of cajoling. Beware, however, the Taurean ruse of allowing themselves to be bribed with sweets; once they've discovered that ruse they'll be bribed by nothing else and another little fatty is set up for life. Better to allow Junior to have his special friend round to play for the afternoon - and all to himself!

SCHOOL AND ONWARDS

Taureans really don't like change so it could be useful in the beginning if there are familiar youngsters starting school at the same time. Once into the strict routine, however, little Taurus should feel comfortable with the predictably repetitive nature of school life. Quite conscientious with school work, albeit a little slow, this youngster should become a reliable and hard working member of the class. They usually concentrate well in learning the basics

and so have the important groundwork that they will need in later life. Perhaps not a top of the class whizzkid but a steady position in class throughout the years. If Junior does fall behind and become pressured it may be necessary for his wellbeing to spend some extra time helping him catch up. Never, though, make it a pressure yourself or you'll have a drop-out on your hands even at this early age! Music and art are very important to Taureans and should be encouraged as much as the more traditional school subjects.

The Three Different Types of Taurus

THE DECANATES

Astrology traditionally divides each of the signs into three equal parts of ten degrees called the decanates. These give a slightly different quality to the sign depending on whether the child is born in the first, second or third ten days of the thirty-day period when one is in a sign. Each third is ruled by one of the three signs in the same element. Taurus is an Earth sign and the three Earth signs are Taurus, Virgo and Capricorn. The nature of Earth signs is basically practical so the following three types each has a different way of expressing their practical abilities.

First Decanate - April 21 to April 30

This is the part of Taurus that is most typical of the sign qualities. Taurus is a builder. The need to improve any raw material with which they work is a basic drive. Whether they are making a home or a garden, a work of art or a career under the Taurean's green fingers, the project just grows and grows. With Venus as the ruling planet, pleasure and beauty are prominent and many Bulls born at this period can become self-indulgent with their need for the good things of life. Often much more romantic than the other two decanates they are attracted to the arts. As small children, encouragement to mould and make things with their hands may have exciting and exceptional results. These small Taureans may become strongly selective not only about their toys but also about the people around them. They seem to have come into this world with good taste and an eye for the best of everything. They won't necessarily all grow up to be art dealers, musical impresarios and business magnates, but you can guarantee that they'll be comfortable and secure with wealthier friends than you've ever had.

Second Decanate - May 1 to May 10

This is the Perfectionist Builder, sharing some of the qualities of Virgo and ruled by quicksilver Mercury. The basic nature of Taurus is to approach all things slowly but carefully building a solid groundwork on which to proceed further. Mercury's influence may speed up this process a little with children born in this decanate. But don't try to make a whizz kid out of this conscientious planner. The Virgo influence gives a much more analytical and thoughtful type of Taurean. They plan ahead and pay great attention to detail in any project that they undertake. Books and information are part of the necessities of life so make sure that Junior has plenty of stimulation in this area. Encouragement to develop the critical faculties in making choices will help fit them for the successful role they will seek later in life. They enjoy discussion and ideas but need to be able to see theories become practical reality.

Third Decanate - May 11 to May 21

The Ambitious Builder ruled by the planet Saturn, this is the tough go-getter of the sign. Almost unlimited patience is brought to bear on any venture that looks like making a reputation. They need to be seen to be successful from the earliest age. Although never fast workers they are thorough and conscientious and will steadily make their ambitious way in schoolwork, achieving respect from their teachers and peers. Often more serious than their small friends they may need to be encouraged to lighten up a little and learn that work is fun. The third decanate also gives a stronger feeling for the value of money and even while quite young, for this little Taurus, the selection of what to buy with pocket money will take on great importance. This is not meanness but a well developed sense of value and in no way conflicts with the natural Taurean good taste. They like the beautiful, and they like it to last!

OTHER LITTLE TAUREANS

Mums and Dads like you delighted in bringing up the following little builders. Yours will probably turn out to be even more famous!

First Decanate Taurus

Queen Elizabeth II, Yehudi Menuhin, William Shakespeare, Shirley Temple, Lee Majors, Sandra Dee, Bernadette Devlin, Shirley MacLaine, Barbra Streisand, Ella Fitzgerald, Samuel Morse, Ulysses S. Grant, Anouk Aimee, Sheena Easton, Duke Ellington.

Second Decanate Taurus

Duke of Wellington, Benjamin Spock, Bing Crosby, Theodore Bikel, Golda Meir, Pete Seeger, Samantha Eggar, Audrey Hepburn, Tammy Wynette, Daniel Gerber, Karl Marx, Sigmund Freud, Rudolf Valentino, Orson Welles, Johannes Brahms, Gary Cooper, Eva Perón.

Third Decanate Taurus

Irving Berlin, Salvador Dali, Mort Sahl, Florence Nightingale, Gabriel Fauré, Susan Hampshire, Joe Louis, Stevie Wonder, George Lucas, Trini Lopez, Liberace, Erik Satie, Pope John Paul II, Ho Chi Minh, Grace Jones, Honoré de Balzac, Moshe Dayan, Albrecht Dürer, Harold Robbins, Cher.

AND NOW THE
PARENTS

THE ARIES PARENT

The good news!

You the Aries parent are energetic, challenging, quick to act, and will immediately experience the 'different' nature of the little Taurean. For Junior is slow but sure and won't be pushed into anything, no matter how enthusiastic or encouraging the parent is, until confident that the tune is right. This relationship personifies 'the tortoise and the hare' and in a competitive situation the Aries parent may be as puzzled as the hare at the outcome. Nevertheless, you share strength of will and a desire to succeed, and will appreciate the steady persistence of the young Bull in overcoming and understanding each facet of a problem in order to reach a successful conclusion. The one  real thing that you have in common is the ability to keep at a challenge until you have it beaten. It's only the time scale that differs. Taureans are slow but never stupid. When you achieve your speedy successes you may not know quite how you did it, but Junior always knows how he did it, he takes the time. Taureans absorb ideas slowly but thoroughly and respond best to firsthand experiment, putting things to practical test and getting the feel of how they work. Aries' belief that 'actions speak louder than words' can fall on receptive ground with this child. Keep the experiments practical and never pressure your little Bull beyond a leisurely pace and you'll enjoy an easy, calm relationship.

...and now the bad news!

Being Aries you know what I'm going to say before I start but the inevitable clash is the old fast/ slow thing. Little Taurus can take a great deal of pushing and shoving before digging in her heels but when she does you have an unsolvable problem on your hands. Irresistible force (Aries) meets immovable object (Taurus) and nobody gets anywhere! How, you may think, can someone so small, so calm and normally so relaxed turn into this red-faced replica of a thick brick wall? Don't do it ! Aries always have to win but this one you won't. If you really subscribe to the 'I did it my way' theme of a true Aries then allow your small Bull to do it his way, very very slowly and even then not until he's ready! If you want to persuade little Taurus to try anything new or unfamiliar then you have to make it fun, make it a pleasure and give plenty of cuddles and you'll never fail.

THE TAURUS PARENT

The good news!

This is an affectionate, cosy relationship with an easy pace and calm atmosphere. Just how young Taurus likes it. You will recognise Junior's need to explore, at leisure, the physical world, taking infinite time and pleasure in this process of discovery. Little Taureans may learn slowly but they certainly learn surely. Though it is unlikely that a calm, patient parent like you would be inclined to rush or push the young Bull, the resulting impasse would soon prove it unwise. This is the most obstinate of all the twelve signs and a conflict between two 'immovable objects' would make the siege interminable. Sharing a great love of home comforts and good living, a little care is necessary in order not to put too much emphasis on self-indulgence. Junior learns by example and though potentially a steady, hard worker the temptations of the easy life are always present. Good routine and familiar patterns of daily life build for little Taurus a surprisingly early self-confidence. Happy to share and take over little responsibilities, this will

do much to increase this down-to-earther's abilities. Though both of you are quite possessive, if you both respect each other's territory all should be well. After all you 'belong' to each other anyway. You'll remember from your own childhood how much you enjoyed doing practical pleasurable things like digging and planting the garden; messy art (finger-painting, mud sculpture etc.) to get the feel of things. Taureans are sensual creatures so don't forget to pass these pleasures on to your little calf; there may be some hidden art talent there!

...and now the bad news!

You both like to take things easy and you both like the good material things of life so here's the problem. The overindulgence can start early with sweeties and cookies as bribes when all else fails. Having acquired a certain plumpness through this easy system, little Taurus is not going to rush out and be sporty especially if Mom or Dad are couch potatoes themselves. The snag is that Taureans are not only happy when they eat, they eat when they're unhappy. The discipline has to start early or the problem can grow to great proportions.

♊

THE GEMINI PARENT

The good news!

If you're the typical Gemini parent then you are eternally young at heart, with a fresh and lively mind that relates well to the childhood world. Your little Taurus will soon dig heels in if the Geminean breakneck pace proves too bewildering. Don't forget to watch out for the signs. After making the interesting discovery that not all quick-thinking Geminis have quick-thinking whizzkids, you'll enthusiastically set about the fascinating business of adapting yourself to a slow-thinking whizzkid.

Taurus is a builder and won't put the roof on, however novel the design, until the walls are completed. In the Gemini household, there'll be no lack of stimulating materials to expand practical young Taurus's 'feel, touch and taste' approach to learning. You should quickly sense that practical experiments work better than theoretical concepts with this youngster. Pressure and too many fingers in too many pies will be met with the immovable

Taurean obstinacy or the Bull's second-string weapon, lethargy (it's too much to do so I won't do anything). Bottom gear on hills for this youngster. Little Taurus can be very creative with the right encouragement and doing things is better than watching things, so start early making music, making models, mud pies, cooking, making a mess, making it tidy, making anything.

...and now the bad news!

You have a sharp fast-thinking approach to life and your quicksilver mind gives you the enviable knack of being able to understand things in a flash. You'll never believe how ponderous the learning process can become with little Taurus and it'll drive you mad if you expect this one to learn in the same way as you did when you were a child. Sad to say, the Geminean love of good snappy back and forth conversation with clever wordplay and wisecracks is hopelessly lost on Junior. Make no mistake, he's not a dimwit, but compared to you little Taurus is almost another species. Taurus builds solid foundations, Gemini tries just enough of everything to get an all-over view of what life is all about. Different roles, different souls. Geminis have the ability to work on several things at the same time and heaven help your little Bull if you don't find another outlet for your speedy wit. Slow down with Junior and you may find that a little extra time spent with your calm relaxed babe may become a little oasis of pleasure in your busy busy life.

THE CANCER PARENT

The good news!

As you know, typical Cancerians are home-loving, family conscious, and sensitive to the material welfare of their children. Little Taurus needs a secure and comfortable home. Both of you have essentially easy-going natures and will share a love of beauty, art, and common sense. You will have no trouble understanding the child's slow, steady way of doing things, and appreciate her necessity to understand and become familiar with each stage of learning before proceeding with the next. To rush young Taureans is to take away the thoroughness with which they build their security. Conflict can occur if Cancer's natural desire to help becomes overprotective and takes over in an attempt to speed things up. Taurus's strong sense of possession will allow sharing but not giving up an anticipated pleasure. Such children need to be respected for standing on their own two feet, and will react with outstanding obstinacy when their sometimes painfully leisurely approach is mistaken for inability. Your little Bull will not willingly explore new experiences, preferring to stay with the familiar and well-tried foods and resisting all attempts at the varied diet that you know he should have. Same with

favourite clothes, you're going to have a few tussles trying to put on Junior's new sweater knitted by Grannie when she next visits! Don't get too upset though for you were probably a little like this when you were a child. You both have a great deal in common and can share with real pleasure, collecting, building and growing things. Both of you are talented in working with your hands, your young Taurean, especially, learns well if encouraged to get the feel of things. Don't fuss if you find the child elbow, or knee deep in water, mud, or custard. The Bull learns through all the senses.

...and now the bad news!

Heaven forbid that there should be any bad news with a Cancerian parent. You're supposed to take to this like a duck to water. However!!! You can be just a teensy weensy bit over protective. If anyone can mollycoddle it's you! Your babe was made for this and will encourage your efforts to protect him or her from the nasty old world outside with positive gurgles of pleasure. Little Taureans can become, under this orgy of parental indulgence, decadent plump little Roman emperors of laziness and self-importance. You'll be making a rod for your own back if you don't resist the typical Cancerian trick of stepping in and helping out, just in case Junior can't manage. Taureans are so slow and leisurely about everything they do, they just seem as though they can't manage things. Wait and see first, you'll be surprised how thoroughly they can do anything if allowed their own pace.

THE LEO PARENT

The good news!

Nobody has to tell you that you're sincere, loving, generous, affectionate and the boss. It's nice to hear it anyway though isn't it? Young Taurus will live in a physically comfortable, nothing-but-the-best, glow of encouragement and high hopes. Your enthusiasm for this grand new venture of parenthood will be contagious and no expense or time will be spared in providing little Taurus with every advantage. The pleasure and luxury will get appreciative response, but no amount of pushing will make the young Bull run before it can walk. The Taurean child is usually industrious with good powers of concentration and a sensitive Leo will admire and encourage the practical talents of this little worker. If these talents are artistic they won't find better support than with a fireball Leo impresario. However, it must be remembered that the little Bull is not such a centre-stage type of being as the old

showbizzy Leo. They prefer to be the solid back-stage support and usually resist the limelight. Leos thrive on appreciation, even from their kids, so if you want to keep things running on a smooth basis think of your little offspring less as an overnight success and more as a small plant that needs lots of sunshine, loads of nourishment and plenty of time to slowly but slowly come into flower. The great thing that you both share is a love of the good things of life and you will be able to encourage and help develop little Taurus's good taste and sense of value in both the material and spiritual worlds.

...and now the bad news!

Leo parents can sometimes be over-enthusiastic and domineering, taking over to such an extent that little Taureans never learn just how strong their own feet are on the ground. Insecure Bulls usually find solace in the larder, become fat and lazy, and that can hit Leo where it hurts. Lions are proud, and appearance matters, 'How could Junior let me down?' The other problem that has the same outcome is that generous old Leo can never refuse to offer second helpings of anything and everything and little Taurus is not the best person in this world to know when she's had enough. If you can resist the temptation to dominate and be over-generous all will be well. Try building the relationship on the projects that you can do together rather than an over-emphasis on the things that you can give each other.

THE VIRGO PARENT

The good news!

Unlike you quick-witted Virgos, little Taurus is slow-thinking, slow-moving and impervious to any attempt at changing this tardy pace. Although sharing your tenacity of purpose in achieving tangible results, this little one's methods differ. The Virgo parent will quickly understand that Junior's way is to experience in physical terms, to gain complete familiarity with the shape, feel, and meaning of each new thing or idea. Steady, but rarely dull, the little Bull's love of the sheer pleasure of play, work, food, toys, Mom and Dad, can fill the cool, orderly Virgoan home with warm, affectionate companionship. For young Taureans, major changes in family life (starting school, moving house, family splits) will require, more than for most, sympathetic help and gentle coaxing in order that they become familiar with, and accept, the new experience. If a dog-eared Teddy has to share the first couple of years at school so be it. Both of you are Earth signs and this means you share an understanding of the practical, material world and need to make a system and routine to keep things running smoothly. Little

Taurus will love the stable efficient ease of your household and will thrive in this perfect environment. Not blessed, however, with your great sense of discipline and willpower, your little Bull may plead for ice cream and sweeties when you're taking him out on a highly educational visit to a natural history museum. You care about health and diet but little Taurus is likely to love all the worst possible things in your book of 'don'ts and nevers'. If anyone can hit a good balance it's you, even if the 'treat' is only once a week on Tuesdays at 3.30. What an organiser!

...and now the bad news!

There may be times when your tidy and analytical Virgoan mind won't be able to resist criticizing Junior's natural lethargy and self-indulgence. This inevitably occurs the moment your back is turned. Let's face it, even if it's for a good reason, you really can be picky! Nag, nag, nag, gets the line of most resistance from this immovably obstinate Bull. This is the opportunity for you to bring into play the brilliant Virgo mind. After all, Virgos are ruled by the planet of intellect, Mercury. The prospect of shared pleasure is a better incentive to move those lazy limbs and you have the wit and inventiveness to provide the projects. Little Taurus loves good, solid building bricks, construction kits, planting and growing seeds and bulbs (window boxes if you don't have a garden), walking in the country, visits to pig styes and palaces, lots of messy paints, mud pies and sand pits. Good earthy stuff!

Ω

THE LIBRA PARENT

The good news!

You take a great deal of pleasure in understanding and relating to the needs of others. Young Taurus's leisurely pace and sensual enjoyment of the colour, shape, touch, and taste of things, will delight your own sensitive, artistic nature. The need for 'thoroughness' is shared by both of you in this relationship. Libra explores every intellectual possibility, and Taurus each material one. This gives the Libra parent a sympathetic approach to Junior's sometimes maddening slowness. The 'giving in' quality of Libra may, in this relationship, need a more than usual balanced view as these two easy-going natures can easily come to a lethargic standstill. The love of harmonious, artistic and beautiful things can provide good creative outlets for getting a little action out of your team. Often surprisingly mature, the little Taurean will take a responsible attitude to school work and helping in the home, excelling in areas where steady effort shows tangible results. Ideas that don't seem to have a material outcome, something that you can feel or see, may not have so great an appeal to this little realist. You can debate for hours the whys, wheres and hows of any project on which you intend to embark. Junior, however, would rather

get his hands messy trying out the practical way with a little less talk and more action. If it often seems like little Taurus just isn't listening, stop talking and get your hands messy too!

...and now the bad news!

In any situation that needs a firm decision, the natural Libran ability to see both sides of any question can negatively lead to taking the easy way out. The easy way out in your case and Junior's is to forget it. Inactivity becomes a favourite occupation and because you're both equally pleasure loving, overindulgence sets in. Don't forget Libra and Taurus are both ruled by the sociable planet Venus, goddess of love and harmony. How did the old masters paint her? Plump and pampered, reclining on a couch peeling a grape or two. Best if both of you get into action on nice cooperative projects. Junior's going to be quite creative with a little Libran stimulation. Get off the old couch and get out the modelling clay, powder paints, paper, scissors, glue, building bricks, pastry, pastry cutters, throw in a musical instrument or two and let another genius loose on the world.

THE SCORPIO PARENT

The good news!

A bit of a cross between a news sleuth and a psychoanalyst, you have an intuitive insight into other people's thoughts and feelings. This natural talent will enable you to easily recognise the importance of the 'slow but sure' method to the little Taurean. The child's response to the sensual world of colour, shape, sound, and the feel of things will be enthusiastically shared and supported. Scorpio is a natural entrepreneur, sensing hidden talents and abilities and nurturing them with the right amount of creative stimulation to produce self-confidence. Little Taurus has a great need for security and this will be well met in the calm strength of the Scorpio parent. Although the Scorpion's protective instinct is powerful, with this child it will take no great sensitivity to know when enough is enough. Little Bulls put out the firmest of signals when they're ready to stand on their own two feet.

It will be a great pleasure to realise that, although a bit of a slow plodder, little Taurus has all the grit and determination to succeed that a typical Scorpion has. This revelation should set up some good supportive deals between the two of you that

will have a lasting effect. You are a very disciplined person and your ability to turn some of the little Bull's over-possessive and self-indulgent pleasure loving ways into positive outlets will pay dividends.

...and now the bad news!

The most obvious cause for clashes with your two signs can come from Scorpio's sometimes domineering manner being met with exasperating Taurean obstinacy. Unfortunately Scorpios, highly emotional as they are, tend to hold in true feelings and resentments with a resulting explosion out of all proportion when they do occasionally let them out for an airing. Little Taurus, normally cool and calm as a cucumber, will not have any of this if she's on the receiving end. Up goes the brick wall and sieges like this can be interminable. Your little Bull won't pull down the barrier until your anger is re-placed with loving cuddles and a quick return to the familiar and comfortable routine that you would be wise to maintain. Although you are opposite signs in the zodiac circle you have a lot in common, both strong and ambitious with the willpower to achieve your aims. Make sure though that you recognise which are yours and which are little Taurus's.

The Sagittarius Parent

The good news!

You are good-humoured, understanding, with a flexible but logical common-sense attitude to young Taurus's welfare. There is little danger that this youngster will feel insecure surrounded by so much optimism. However, Sagittarians usually hate routine or being tied down in any way so the little Taurean's lack of pace may sometimes try the Archer's patience. Once it is established that Junior, although slow and thorough, develops an early sense of independence through familiarity with predictable routines, a good compromise can be reached. Sagittarians treat children as intelligent human beings, refusing to cajole, tell white lies or put off with 'when you're older, dear'. Simple, honest answers to any question give young Taureans the solid background of practical knowledge that develops self-confidence and individuality. They need to know exactly how things are with no beating about the bush and you, as a truth-loving Sagittarian, will always let your little Bull know just that. You rarely waste time hiding what you feel and let those around you know exactly what you think when you think it! Little Taurus is firmly based in the present, preferring to dwell on what's going

on now and resisting any real change to the status quo. Sagittarius's natural being is optimistic and far-seeing, always looking for pastures new, so you can see that there will have to be a little guile and cunning if you're going to get Junior to move on and share the next pleasurable experience with you.

...and now the bad news!

The biggest threat to the relationship is that your Sagittarian temperament, always on the move, can become distant, preoccupied, or just not around when needed. This can bring out the more possessive, demanding nature of little Taurus and so inflate the very situation that you as a freedom loving Centaur wish to avoid. This symbolic beast, half human, half spirited horse, needs to roam free and unhampered and doesn't take kindly to being tethered at home to a child that doesn't want to go anywhere! If you get into that situation it'll be your own making. Best that you start really early taking this little 'stick in the mud' with you on a few of your adventures. Once little Taurus knows where you go and what you do when you're not with her it's filed away in her little book of realities and the problem is almost over. But you'll have to keep working on it. Country walks are a must. Taureans love the earth and to be surrounded by green and growing things is one of their great pleasures, even if it means travelling to unfamiliar territory.

THE CAPRICORN PARENT

The good news!

You are one of the most conscientious and supportive parents, and will certainly provide the comfortable background of well-organized routine in which young Taureans thrive. Though ambitious for Junior's achievements, you are endowed with unlimited patience and sense of purpose, relating easily to little Taurus's need for thoroughness that often will make his progress seem painfully slow. Pushed too far and too fast, little Bulls become timid and insecure, yet can be surprisingly .quick in showing self-reliance in areas where they have been given the time to completely familiarize themselves. In anything they do they have to be thorough and as this is second nature to the ambitious Capricorn as well, the two of you should have no problems here. All this conscientiousness can sound a little dull and in truth you may get somewhat bogged down in routine so that everything gets too predictable. Little Bulls love pleasurable things and are essentially romantic little beings so

spice up this relationship with plenty of fun. Surprises are pleasant if not too outrageously different and not too unexpected. Junior is not the over adventurous type. Best of all, the affectionate little Taurean responds positively to, and needs plenty of, hugs and kisses, even their natural obstinacy melting with copious doses of physical warmth.

...and now the bad news!

'How can this perfect twin Earth sign combination not get on?' you may say. The trouble is that you could get on almost too well. In too easy an atmosphere, without a real challenge, little Taurus's love of the sense-world can lead him to lazy self-indulgence and stubborn inactivity. Slow paced, the little Bull rarely works off results of the long stay at the lunch table as their little hyperactive friends do. This, combined with a love of the stodgy, the sweet and the fried in the way of food, may cause you and your little 'fatty' Taurus a few problems. When this provokes the worst of Capricorn's 'lecturing' potential, Junior's stubbornness knows no bounds. Good subtle weaning off the sweet and the sticky early on will pay dividends. Happily, unsolvable battles are few in this well-matched common-sense relationship.

The Aquarius Parent

The good news!

Like most Aquarians you'll approach parenthood with an open mind and a good knack for making unusual methods work. This avant-garde outlook may suffer a few initial setbacks when confronted by a stubborn little Taurean. In no uncertain terms, this solid little creature of habit will make it known that the only acceptable way to bring up a Bull is by routine. Although rigid routines in terms of the material chores of life are not your favourite occupation you are quite organised when it comes to thought. Striking a balance between your slightly unorthodox approach and Junior's desire for the ordinary and familiar will be a constant challenge. Little Taurus will respond to your freethinking methods as long as the basic ideas, however 'different', are regularly maintained. The bonus for making a concession in this area will be young Taurus's surprisingly early self-reliance. Although they tend to take everything with a much more measured approach it shows it's worth later,

in a surprisingly confident approach to school work. Your child will never be punished for telling the truth, no matter how shocking. Aquarians always treat their children with respect and a friendly trust that encourages honest self-expression. Your love of company will produce a busy household with much coming and going of friends and colleagues. This could be a great help to counter the unadventurous nature of your little Bull. Make sure though that Junior gets brought into the conversation and is never, no matter how young, left out in the cold. Taureans are unbelievably possessive when life looks a little less secure.

...and now the bad news!

It's obvious from the above that too much sudden, new and unusual stimuli can throw the little Taurean into helpless confusion. What may seem to be great new stimulus to your little one's creative development can have adverse results with this small creature of habit. An insecure, possessive child is the freedom-loving Aquarian's worst threat. You love company, but on your terms, and that isn't to have a clinging, stubborn, podgy little Taurus refusing to let you get out of sight or out of earshot. Taurus thrives on rules and even eccentric Aquarian ones can work if you stick to 'em. If you're that rare being, a huggin' and kissin' Aquarian, good at physical contact, then great for little cuddly Taurus! If not, give it a try, it works wonders when Junior is at her most obstinate.

THE PISCES PARENT

The good news!

Although not a natural stickler for routine you will sensitively feel little Taurus's need for well-ordered schedules and predictable patterns. Rarely forgetting the deep impressions of their own childhood, Pisceans easily sense the feelings and needs of their small charges. The little Bull's approach to learning can be a pleasure to observe. Everyday objects are felt, fumbled, stroked, tasted and thumped into familiarity. New distractions are ignored or stubbornly refused until this thorough exploration is complete. The Piscean talent for fantasy and storytelling can expand the imaginative side of this little realist. Magical fairyland exploits, however, may fall on stony ground in favour of the more earthy adventures of tractors and trains. Often developing early independence, Junior will still need oceans of Piscean affection. The most obstinate Taurean tantrum melts easily with a warm loving hug. Your little Bull can't ever get enough of the cuddling side of this relationship but all your sensitivity may come to a halt when confronted with

the other side of the little Taurus character. 'Digging the heels in!' is something almost unknown to the gentle and adaptable Pisces but second nature to Junior. Pisces, when confronted by an immovable object, like the water element that your sign represents, will just flow around the difficulty. How you do this successfully only you can know, but the Piscean ability to produce attractive alternative ideas at the drop of a hat should help carry little Taurus out of his most obstinate standoff without him even noticing what's happened.

...and now the bad news!

The selfless Piscean need to 'give' can, if taken to extremes, bring out Junior's worst potential: inaction. Luxury-loving, self-indulgent and probably fat (Taurean sins go quickly to the waistline) your little one can become a big, big problem. You break all the rules as soon as you've made them so how can your little Taurus even begin to know where she stands. Threats are no good, no matter how inventive, if you don't stand a hope of carrying them out and one thing Junior's going to learn very quickly is that you're the softest touch in the zodiac. Loving parent as you undoubtedly are, this won't help your little one at all. Keep the routine regular, young Taurus on the move and share lots of creative pursuits with plenty of varied materials (paint, clay, pastry etc.); dance (music can get this little one moving); helping with responsible little jobs; toy cookers, vacuum cleaners, shops, woodwork sets (the more like the real thing, the better).

ON THE CUSP

Many people whose children are born on the day the sun changes signs are not sure whether they come under one sign or another. Some say one is supposed to be a little bit of each but this is rarely true. Adjoining signs are very different to each other so checking up can make everything clear. The opposite table gives the exact Greenwich Mean Time (GMT) when the sun moves into Taurus and when it leaves. Subtract or add the hours indicated below for your nearest big city.

AMSTERDAM	GMT + 01.00	MADRID	GMT + 01.00
ATHENS	GMT + 02.00	MELBOURNE	GMT + 10.00
BOMBAY	GMT + 05.30	MONTREAL	GMT - 05.00
CAIRO	GMT + 02.00	NEW YORK	GMT - 05.00
CALGARY	GMT - 07.00	PARIS	GMT + 01.00
CHICAGO	GMT - 06.00	ROME	GMT + 01.00
DURBAN	GMT + 02.00	S.FRANCISCO	GMT - 08.00
GIBRALTAR	GMT + 01.00	SYDNEY	GMT + 10.00
HOUSTON	GMT - 06.00	TOKYO	GMT + 09.00
LONDON	GMT 00.00	WELLINGTON	GMT + 12.00

DATE	ENTERS TAURUS	GMT	LEAVES TAURUS	GMT
1984	APR 19	9.38 PM	MAY 20	8.58 PM
1985	APR 20	3.26 AM	MAY 21	2.43 AM
1986	APR 20	9.12 AM	MAY 21	8.28 AM
1987	APR 20	2.57 PM	MAY 21	2.10 PM
1988	APR 19	8.45 PM	MAY 20	7.57 PM
1989	APR 20	2.39 AM	MAY 21	1.53 AM
1990	APR 20	8.26 AM	MAY 21	7.37 AM
1991	APR 20	2.09 PM	MAY 21	1.20 PM
1992	APR 19	7.57 PM	MAY 20	7.12 PM
1993	APR 20	1.49 AM	MAY 21	1.01 AM
1994	APR 20	7.36 AM	MAY 21	6.48 AM
1995	APR 20	1.21 PM	MAY 21	12.34 PM
1996	APR 19	7.10 PM	MAY 20	6.23 PM
1997	APR 20	1.03 AM	MAY 21	12.18 AM
1998	APR 20	6.57 AM	MAY 21	6.05 AM
1999	APR 20	12.46 PM	MAY 21	11.53 AM
2000	APR 19	6.39 PM	MAY 20	5.49 PM
2001	APR 20	12.36 AM	MAY 21	11.44 AM
2002	APR 20	6.21 AM	MAY 21	5.30 AM
2003	APR 20	12.03 PM	MAY 21	11.13 AM
2004	APR19	5.15 PM	MAY 20	4.59 PM

John Astrop is an astrologer and author, has written and illustrated over two hundred books for children, is a little Scorpio married to a little Cancerian artist, has one little Capricorn psychologist, one little Pisces songwriter, one little Virgo traveller and a little Aries rock guitarist. The cats are little Sagittarians.